Macarons

MARIE-LAURE TOMBINI

hinkler

Contents

Guava macarons

Makes 15 to 20 small macarons
Preparation: 30 min
Cooking time: 17 min
Rest mixture: 1 h

120 g (4¼ oz) of icing sugar (confectioner's sugar)

80 g (2¾ oz) of almond flour

2 egg whites (80 g/2¾ oz)

1 pinch of salt (optional)

60 g (2 oz) of castor sugar (berry sugar)

1 pinch of orange-pink powdered food colouring (colouring agent)

For guava cream:

100 ml (3½ fl oz) of guava juice

1 egg yolk (20 g/⅔ oz)

10 g (⅓ oz) of cornflour (cornstarch)

40 g (1½ oz) of castor sugar (berry sugar)

1 pinch of orange-pink powdered food colouring (colouring agent)

1. Make macaron shells according to the basic recipe (see p. 62).
2. Prepare guava cream: in a bowl, mix the cornflour (cornstarch) gradually with guava juice. Add beaten egg yolk and castor sugar (berry sugar). Beat vigorously.
3. Transfer the mixture to a saucepan and cook for about 5 minutes on medium heat, stirring constantly, until cream thickens. Add the food colouring (colouring agent).
4. Pour the cream into a bowl, cover with plastic wrap and let cool to room temperature.
5. To assemble garnish 1 macaron shell with guava cream then cover with another shell. Assemble remaining macarons accordingly.

Passionfruit-basil macarons

Makes 15 to 20 small macarons
Preparation: 30 min
Cooking time: 17 min
Rest mixture: 1 h

120 g (4¼ oz) of icing sugar (confectioner's sugar)

80 g (2¾ oz) of almond flour

2 egg whites (80 g/2¾ oz)

1 pinch of salt (optional)

60 g (2 oz) of castor sugar (berry sugar)

1 pinch of green-yellow powdered food colouring (colouring agent)

For passionfruit-basil cream:

1 passionfruit

80 ml (2¾ fl oz) of passionfruit juice

1 egg yolk (20 g/⅔ oz)

8 g (¼ oz) of cornflour (cornstarch)

20 g (⅔ oz) of castor sugar (berry sugar)

1 drop of basil essential oil (available from health food stores)

1. Make macaron shells according to the basic recipe (see p. 62).
2. Prepare passionfruit-basil cream: in a bowl, mix the cornflour (cornstarch) gradually with passionfruit juice. Add beaten egg yolk and castor sugar (berry sugar). Beat vigorously.
3. Transfer the mixture to a saucepan and cook for about 5 minutes on medium heat, stirring constantly, until cream thickens.
4. Remove from heat, mix in the passionfruit flesh and basil essential oil.
5. Pour the cream into a bowl, cover with plastic wrap and let cool to room temperature.
6. To assemble garnish 1 macaron shell with passionfruit-basil cream and then cover with another shell. Assemble remaining macarons accordingly.

Nectarine-apricot macarons

Makes 15 to 20 small macarons
Preparation: 30 min
Cooking time: 30 min
Rest mixture: 1 h

120 g (4¼ oz) of icing sugar (confectioner's sugar)

80 g (2¾ oz) of almond flour

2 egg whites (80 g/2¾ oz)

1 pinch of salt (optional)

60 g (2 oz) of castor sugar (berry sugar)

1 pinch of orange powdered food colouring (colouring agent)

For nectarine-apricot stewed fruit:

1 nectarine (120 g/4¼ oz)

4 apricots (150 g/5¼ oz)

1 pinch of powdered cardamom

60 g (2 oz) of castor sugar (berry sugar)

1. Make macaron shells according to the basic recipe (see p. 62).
2. Prepare stewed fruit: cut flesh of the fruits into small diced pieces. Put them in a pan, sprinkle with castor sugar (berry sugar) and warm on medium heat. As soon as steam is released, cover, lower the heat and cook for about 15–20 minutes, stirring occasionally. If you think the stewed fruit is cooked but still slightly liquid, let it reduce without cover while stirring.
3. Remove from heat, add cardamom and allow to cool.
4. To assemble garnish 1 macaron shell with stewed fruit then cover with another shell. Assemble remaining macarons accordingly.

Gooseberry macarons

Makes 15 to 20 small macarons
Preparation: 30 min
Cooking time: 20 min
Rest mixture: 1 h

120 g (4¼ oz) of icing sugar (confectioner's sugar)

80 g (2¾ oz) of almond flour

2 egg whites (80 g/2¾ oz)

1 pinch of salt (optional)

60 g (2 oz) of castor sugar (berry sugar)

1 pinch of pink powdered food colouring (colouring agent)

For gooseberry jam:

70 g (2½ oz) of gooseberry (alma) juice (available from health food stores)

70 g (2½ oz) of gelling sugar (jam or jelly sugar)

1. Make macaron shells according to the basic recipe (see p. 62).
2. Prepare gooseberry jam: mix gooseberry (alma) juice and gelling sugar (jam or jelly sugar) in a saucepan. Heat the mixture and bring to boil. Cook for 5–7 minutes on high heat, stirring constantly.
3. Pour the jam into a jar and allow to cool.
4. To assemble garnish 1 macaron shell with gooseberry jam then cover with another shell. Assemble remaining macarons accordingly.

Violet-blackcurrant macarons

Makes 15 to 20 small macarons
Preparation: 20 min
Cooking time: 15 min
Rest mixture: 1 h

120 g (4¼ oz) of icing sugar (confectioner's sugar)

80 g (2¾ oz) of almond flour

2 egg whites (80 g/2¾ oz)

1 pinch of salt (optional)

60 g (2 oz) of castor sugar (berry sugar)

1 pinch of violet powdered food colouring (colouring agent)

For ganache:

100 g (3½ oz) of white chocolate

50 g (1¾ oz) of fresh blackcurrants

30 g (1 oz) of heavy whipping cream

1 teaspoon of violet essence (available from specialty baking stores)

1. Make macaron shells according to the basic recipe (see p. 62).
2. Prepare ganache: in a saucepan melt chocolate with cream on low heat. Add violet essence.
3. Blend the mixture with blackcurrants and allow mixture to cool to room temperature.
4. To assemble garnish 1 macaron shell with ganache then cover with another shell. Assemble remaining macarons accordingly.

Lime macarons

Makes 15 to 20 small macarons
Preparation: 30 min
Cooking time: 17 min
Rest mixture: 1 h

120 g (4¼ oz) of icing sugar (confectioner's sugar)

80 g (2¾ oz) of almond flour

2 egg whites (80 g/2¾ oz)

1 pinch of salt (optional)

60 g (2 oz) of castor sugar (berry sugar)

1 pinch of green powdered food colouring (colouring agent)

For lime cream:

100 ml (3½ fl oz) of lime juice

1 egg

10 g (⅓ oz) of cornflour (cornstarch)

50 g (1¾ oz) of castor sugar (berry sugar)

1. Make macaron shells according to the basic recipe (see p. 62).
2. Prepare lime cream: in a bowl, mix the cornflour (cornstarch) gradually with lime juice. Add beaten egg and castor sugar (berry sugar). Beat vigorously.
3. Transfer the mixture to a saucepan and cook for about 5 minutes on medium heat, stirring constantly, until cream thickens.
4. Pour the cream into a bowl, cover with plastic wrap and let cool to room temperature.
5. To assemble garnish 1 macaron shell with lime cream then cover with another shell. Assemble remaining macarons accordingly.

Chocolate-coconut macarons

Makes 15 to 20 small macarons
Preparation: 30 min
Cooking time: 15 min
Rest mixture: 1 h

120 g (4¼ oz) of icing sugar (confectioner's sugar)

80 g (2¾ oz) of almond flour

2 tablespoons (6 teaspoons) of unsweetened cocoa powder

2 egg whites (80 g/2¾ oz)

1 pinch of salt (optional)

60 g (2 oz) of castor sugar (berry sugar)

For ganache:

100 g (3½ oz) of dark chocolate (semi-sweet chocolate)

50 ml (1⅗ fl oz) of coconut milk

30 g (1 oz) of grated coconut

1. Make macaron shells according to the basic recipe (see p. 62), mixing cocoa with almond flour and icing sugar (confectioner's sugar) in first step.
2. Prepare ganache: in a saucepan melt the chocolate with coconut milk on low heat.
3. Add grated coconut and allow mixture to cool to room temperature.
4. To assemble garnish 1 macaron shell with ganache and then cover with another shell. Assemble remaining macarons accordingly.

Grapefruit and orange flower macarons

Makes 15 to 20 small macarons
Preparation: 30 min
Cooking time: 17 min
Rest mixture: 1 h

120 g (4¼ oz) of icing sugar (confectioner's sugar)

80 g (2¾ oz) of almond flour

2 egg whites (80 g/2¾ oz)

1 pinch of salt (optional)

60 g (2 oz) of castor sugar (berry sugar)

1 pinch of orange powdered food colouring (colouring agent)

For grapefruit cream:

100 ml (3½ fl oz) of grapefruit juice

1 egg

80 g (2¾ oz) of castor sugar (berry sugar)

10 g (⅓ oz) of cornflour (cornstarch)

1 tablespoon (3 teaspoons) of orange flower water (available from delicatessens)

1. Make macaron shells according to the basic recipe (see p. 62).
2. Prepare grapefruit cream: in a bowl, mix cornflour (cornstarch) and castor sugar (berry sugar). Dilute with grapefruit juice. Add beaten egg and mix well.
3. Transfer the mixture to a saucepan and cook for 5 minutes on medium heat, whisking constantly until cream thickens. Stir in orange flower water.
4. Pour the cream into a bowl, cover with plastic wrap and let cool to room temperature.
5. To assemble garnish 1 macaron shell with grapefruit cream then cover with another shell. Assemble remaining macarons accordingly.

Lavender macarons

Makes 15 to 20 small macarons
Preparation: 30 min
Cooking time: 17 min
Rest mixture: 1 h

120 g (4¼ oz) of icing sugar (confectioner's sugar)
80 g (2¾ oz) of almond flour
2 egg whites (80 g/2¾ oz)
1 pinch of salt (optional)
60 g (2 oz) of castor sugar (berry sugar)
1 pinch of violet powdered food colouring (colouring agent)

For lavender cream:

100 ml (3½ fl oz) of lukewarm milk
1 egg yolk (20 g/⅔ oz)
10 g (⅓ oz) of cornflour (cornstarch)
25 g (¾ oz) of castor sugar (berry sugar)
40 g (1½ oz) of softened butter
1 or 2 drops of lavender essential oil (available from health food stores)
1 pinch of violet powdered food colouring (colouring agent)

1. Make macaron shells according to the basic recipe (see p. 62).
2. Prepare lavender cream: in a bowl, mix cornflour (cornstarch) and castor sugar (berry sugar). Add the egg yolk and beat vigorously. Stir in the lukewarm milk.
3. Transfer the mixture to a saucepan and cook for about 5 minutes on medium heat, stirring constantly, until cream thickens.
4. Remove from heat, add butter, lavender essential oil and the food colouring (colouring agent). Mix everything well.
5. Pour the cream into a bowl, cover with plastic wrap and let cool to room temperature.
6. To assemble garnish 1 macaron shell with lavender cream then cover with another shell. Assemble remaining macarons accordingly.

Salted butter caramel macarons

Makes 15 to 20 small macarons
Preparation: 30 min
Cooking time: 20 min
Rest mixture: 1 h

120 g (4¼ oz) of icing sugar (confectioner's sugar)

80 g (2¾ oz) of almond flour

5 g (⅙ oz) of unsweetened cocoa powder

2 egg whites (80 g/2¾ oz)

1 pinch of salt (optional)

60 g (2 oz) of castor sugar (berry sugar)

1 pinch of yellow powdered food colouring (colouring agent)

For salted butter caramel:

50 g (1¾ oz) of castor sugar (berry sugar)

20 g (⅔ oz) of low-salt butter (half-salted butter)

100 ml (3½ fl oz) of heavy whipping cream

1. Make macaron shells according to the basic recipe (see p. 62), mixing cocoa with almond flour and icing sugar (confectioner's sugar) in first step.
2. Prepare salted butter caramel: heat the castor sugar (berry sugar) in a stainless steel saucepan on medium heat and cook without stirring until it is melted and caramelised. Slowly add low-salt butter (half-salted butter) and then the cream while stirring briskly with a whisk to avoid lumps. When the mixture is smooth, continue cooking for 5 minutes and remove from heat.
3. Pour the caramel into a bowl and allow to cool.
4. To assemble garnish 1 macaron shell with salted butter caramel and then cover with another shell. Assemble remaining macarons accordingly.

Strawberry macarons

Makes 15 to 20 small macarons
Preparation: 30 min
Cooking time: 15 min
Rest mixture: 1 h

120 g (4¼ oz) of icing sugar (confectioner's sugar)

80 g (2¾ oz) of almond flour

2 egg whites (80 g/2¾ oz)

1 pinch of salt (optional)

60 g (2 oz) of castor sugar (berry sugar)

1 pinch of pink powdered food colouring (colouring agent)

For ganache:

100 g (3½ oz) of white chocolate

50 g (1¾ oz) of strawberry puree

30 ml (1 fl oz) of heavy whipping cream

1. Make macaron shells according to the basic recipe (see p. 62).
2. Prepare ganache: in a saucepan melt chocolate with cream on low heat.
3. Add strawberry puree and allow mixture to cool to room temperature.
4. To assemble garnish 1 macaron shell with chocolate-strawberry ganache and then cover with another shell. Assemble remaining macarons accordingly.

Chocolate and tonka bean macarons

Makes 15 to 20 small macarons
Preparation: 25 min
Cooking time: 15 min
Rest mixture: 1 h

120 g (4¼ oz) of icing sugar (confectioner's sugar)

80 g (2¾ oz) of almond flour

2 egg whites (80 g/2¾ oz)

1 pinch of salt (optional)

60 g (2 oz) of castor sugar (berry sugar)

1 pinch of black powdered food colouring (colouring agent)

For ganache:

100 g (3½ oz) of dark chocolate (semi-sweet chocolate)

½ tonka bean (can be found in specialty baking stores, alternatively, substitute ½ teaspoon of vanilla and ¼ teaspoon of almond extracts)

50 ml (1⅗ fl oz) of heavy whipping cream

1. Make macaron shells according to the basic recipe (see p. 62).
2. Prepare ganache: in a saucepan melt chocolate with cream on low heat.
3. Add grated ½ tonka bean and allow mixture to cool to room temperature.
4. To assemble garnish 1 macaron shell with ganache and then cover with another shell. Assemble remaining macarons accordingly.

Pistachio macarons

Makes 15 to 20 small macarons
Preparation: 30 min
Cooking time: 17 min
Rest mixture: 1 h

120 g (4¼ oz) of icing sugar (confectioner's sugar)

80 g (2¾ oz) of almond flour

2 egg whites (80 g/2¾ oz)

1 pinch of salt (optional)

60 g (2 oz) of castor sugar (berry sugar)

1 pinch of green powdered food colouring (colouring agent)

For pistachio cream:

100 ml (3½ fl oz) of lukewarm milk

1 egg yolk (20 g/⅔ oz)

25 g (¾ oz) of castor sugar (berry sugar)

12 g (⅖ oz) of cornflour (cornstarch)

25 g (¾ oz) of finely chopped pistachios

1. Make macaron shells according to the basic recipe (see p. 62).
2. Prepare pistachio cream: in a bowl, mix cornflour (cornstarch) and castor sugar (berry sugar). Add the egg yolk and beat vigorously. Stir in the lukewarm milk.
3. Transfer the mixture to a saucepan and cook for about 5 minutes on medium heat, whisking constantly until cream thickens. Add chopped pistachios.
4. Pour the cream into a bowl, cover with plastic wrap and let cool to room temperature.
5. To assemble garnish 1 macaron shell with pistachio cream and then cover with another shell. Assemble remaining macarons accordingly.

Hazelnut macarons

Makes 15 to 20 small macarons
Preparation: 30 min
Cooking time: 17 min
Rest mixture: 1 h

120 g ($4\frac{1}{4}$ oz) of icing sugar (confectioner's sugar)

80 g ($2\frac{3}{4}$ oz) of hazelnut flour

5 g ($\frac{1}{6}$ oz) of unsweetened cocoa powder

2 egg whites (80 g/$2\frac{3}{4}$ oz)

1 pinch of salt (optional)

60 g (2 oz) of castor sugar (berry sugar)

For hazelnut cream:

80 ml ($2\frac{3}{4}$ fl oz) of lukewarm milk

1 egg yolk (20 g/$\frac{2}{3}$ oz)

10 g ($\frac{1}{3}$ oz) of cornflour (cornstarch)

10 g ($\frac{1}{3}$ oz) of castor sugar (berry sugar)

25 g ($\frac{3}{4}$ oz) of hazelnut flour

20 g ($\frac{2}{3}$ oz) of softened butter

1. Make macaron shells according to the basic recipe (see p. 62), mixing cocoa with hazelnut flour and icing sugar (confectioner's sugar) in first step.
2. Prepare hazelnut cream: in a bowl, mix cornflour (cornstarch) and castor sugar (berry sugar). Add the egg yolk and beat vigorously. Stir in the lukewarm milk.
3. Transfer the mixture to a saucepan and cook for about 5 minutes on medium heat, stirring constantly, until cream thickens.
4. Remove from heat, add butter and hazelnut flour.
5. Pour the cream into a bowl, cover with plastic wrap and let cool to room temperature.
6. To assemble garnish 1 macaron shell with hazelnut cream and then cover with another shell. Assemble remaining macarons accordingly.

Orange and poppy seed macarons

Makes 15 to 20 small macarons
Preparation: 20 min
Cooking time: 17 min
Rest mixture: 1 h

120 g (4¼ oz) of icing sugar (confectioner's sugar)

80 g (2¾ oz) of almond flour

2 egg whites (80 g/2¾ oz)

1 pinch of salt (optional)

20 g (⅔ oz) of castor sugar (berry sugar)

1 pinch of orange powdered food colouring (colouring agent)

For orange cream:

1 egg

100 ml (3½ fl oz) of orange juice

60 g (2 oz) of castor sugar (berry sugar)

10 g (⅓ oz) of cornflour (cornstarch)

1 tablespoon (3 teaspoons) of poppy seeds

1. Make macaron shells according to the basic recipe (see p. 62).
2. Prepare orange cream: in a bowl mix cornflour (cornstarch) and castor sugar (berry sugar). Dilute with orange juice. Add beaten egg and mix well.
3. Transfer the mixture to a saucepan and cook for about 5 minutes on medium heat, whisking constantly until cream thickens. Stir in the poppy seeds.
4. Pour the cream into a bowl, cover with plastic wrap and let cool to room temperature.
5. To assemble garnish 1 macaron shell with orange cream and then cover with another shell. Assemble remaining macarons accordingly.

Lemon-saffron macarons

Makes 15 to 20 small macarons
Preparation: 20 min
Cooking time: 17 min
Rest mixture: 1 h

120 g (4¼ oz) of icing sugar (confectioner's sugar)

80 g (2¾ oz) of almond flour

2 egg whites (80 g/2¾ oz)

1 pinch of salt (optional)

60 g (2 oz) of castor sugar (berry sugar)

1 pinch of yellow powdered food colouring (colouring agent)

For lemon cream:

1 egg

100 ml (3½ fl oz) of lemon juice

60 g (2 oz) of castor sugar (berry sugar)

10 g (⅓ oz) of cornflour (cornstarch)

½ pod of powdered saffron

1. Make macaron shells according to the basic recipe (see p. 62).
2. Prepare lemon cream: in a bowl mix cornflour (cornstarch) and castor sugar (berry sugar). Dilute with lemon juice. Add beaten egg and mix well.
3. Transfer the mixture to a saucepan and cook for about 5 minutes on medium heat, whisking constantly until cream thickens. Stir in saffron.
4. Pour the cream into a bowl, cover with plastic wrap and let cool to room temperature.
5. To assemble garnish 1 macaron shell with lemon cream and then cover with another shell. Assemble remaining macarons accordingly.

My advice: lemon cream keeps for 4 days in refrigerator.

Curaçao macarons

Makes 15 to 20 small macarons
Preparation: 30 min
Cooking time: 17 min
Rest mixture: 1 h

120 g (4¼ oz) of icing sugar (confectioner's sugar)

80 g (2¾ oz) of almond flour

2 egg whites (80 g/2¾ oz)

1 pinch of salt (optional)

60 g (2 oz) of castor sugar (berry sugar)

1 pinch of blue powdered food colouring (colouring agent)

For Curaçao cream:

100 ml (3½ fl oz) of lukewarm milk

1 egg yolk (20 g/⅔ oz)

10 g (⅓ oz) of cornflour (cornstarch)

25 g (¾ oz) of castor sugar (berry sugar)

2 tablespoons (6 teaspoons) of Curaçao liqueur

1. Make macaron shells according to the basic recipe (see p. 62).
2. Prepare Curaçao cream: in a bowl mix cornflour (cornstarch) and castor sugar (berry sugar). Add the egg yolk and beat vigorously. Stir in the lukewarm milk.
3. Transfer the mixture to a saucepan and cook for about 5 minutes on medium heat, stirring constantly, until cream thickens. Add Curaçao liqueur.
4. Pour the cream into a bowl, cover with plastic wrap and let cool to room temperature.
5. To assemble garnish 1 macaron shell with Curaçao cream and then cover with another shell. Assemble remaining macarons accordingly.

Vanilla macarons

Makes 15 to 20 small macarons
Preparation: 30 min
Cooking time: 17 min
Rest mixture: 1 h

120 g (4¼ oz) of icing sugar (confectioner's sugar)

80 g (2¾ oz) of almond flour

2 egg whites (80 g/2¾ oz)

1 pinch of salt (optional)

60 g (2 oz) of castor sugar (berry sugar)

For vanilla cream:

100 ml (3½ fl oz) of lukewarm milk

1 egg yolk (20 g/⅔ oz)

25 g (¾ oz) of castor sugar (berry sugar)

12 g (⅖ oz) of cornflour (cornstarch)

1 vanilla pod

1. Make macaron shells according to the basic recipe (see p. 62), without adding food colouring (colouring agent).
2. Prepare vanilla cream: in a bowl mix cornflour (cornstarch) and castor sugar (berry sugar). Add the egg yolk and beat vigorously. Stir in the lukewarm milk, and the split and scraped vanilla pod.
3. Transfer the mixture to a saucepan and cook for about 5 minutes on medium heat, whisking constantly until cream thickens.
4. Pour the cream into a bowl, cover with plastic wrap and let cool to room temperature.
5. To assemble garnish 1 macaron shell with vanilla cream and then cover with another shell. Assemble remaining macarons accordingly.

My advice: these macarons taste best when served 12 to 24 hours after being made.

Dark chocolate and chestnut macarons

Makes 15 to 20 small macarons
Preparation: 30 min
Cooking time: 15 min
Rest mixture: 1 h

120 g (4¼ oz) of icing sugar (confectioner's sugar)

80 g (2¾ oz) of almond flour

2 tablespoons (6 teaspoons) of unsweetened cocoa powder

2 egg whites (80 g/2¾ oz)

1 pinch of salt (optional)

60 g (2 oz) of castor sugar (berry sugar)

For ganache:

50 g (1¾ oz) of chestnut cream

50 g (1¾ oz) of dark chocolate (semi-sweet chocolate)

1 tablespoon (3 teaspoons) of heavy whipping cream

1. Make macaron shells according to the basic recipe (see p. 62), mixing the cocoa with almond flour and icing sugar (confectioner's sugar) in first step.
2. Prepare ganache: in a saucepan melt the chocolate, broken into pieces, with the heavy whipping cream on low heat.
3. Remove from heat, stir in chestnut cream. Let the ganache cool to room temperature.
4. To assemble garnish 1 macaron shell with ganache and then cover with another shell. Assemble remaining macarons accordingly.

My advice: Chestnut cream is available from delicatessens. It can also be made by adding a teaspoon of chestnut puree to 50 g (1¾ oz) of whipped cream.

Fig macarons

Makes 15 to 20 small macarons
Preparation: 30 min
Cooking time: 20 min
Rest mixture: 1 h

120 g (4¼ oz) of icing sugar (confectioner's sugar)

80 g (2¾ oz) of almond flour

2 egg whites (80 g/2¾ oz)

1 pinch of salt (optional)

60 g (2 oz) of castor sugar (berry sugar)

1 pinch of violet powdered food colouring (colouring agent)

For fig jam:

200 g (7 oz) of fresh figs

50 g (1¾ oz) of gelling sugar (jam or jelly sugar)

1 tablespoon (3 teaspoons) of lemon juice

1. Make macaron shells according to the basic recipe (see p. 62).
2. Prepare jam: peel the figs and cut them into pieces. Put them in a saucepan with gelling sugar (jam or jelly sugar) and lemon juice. Mix and bring to boil by heating on high heat. Cook for 5–7 minutes while stirring constantly.
3. Let the jam cool to room temperature.
4. To assemble garnish 1 macaron shell with fig jam and then cover with another shell. Assemble remaining macarons accordingly.

Rose macarons

Makes 15 to 20 small macarons
Preparation: 30 min
Cooking time: 12 min
Rest mixture: 1 h

120 g (4¼ oz) of icing sugar (confectioner's sugar)

80 g (2¾ oz) of almond flour

2 egg whites (80 g/2¾ oz)

1 pinch of salt (optional)

60 g (2 oz) of castor sugar (berry sugar)

1 pinch of pink powdered food colouring (colouring agent)

For rose cream:

100 g (3½ oz) of cream cheese

30 g (1 oz) of icing sugar (confectioner's sugar)

1 tablespoon (3 teaspoons) of rosewater

1 pinch of pink powdered food colouring (colouring agent)

1. Make macaron shells according to the basic recipe (see p. 62).
2. Prepare rose cream: in a bowl mix icing sugar (confectioner's sugar) and rosewater. Stir in cream cheese. Add the food colouring (colouring agent) and mix well. Cover the rose cream with plastic wrap and refrigerate if you do not use it immediately.
3. To assemble garnish 1 macaron shell with rose cream and then cover with another shell. Assemble remaining macarons accordingly.

Banana and white chocolate macarons

Makes 15 to 20 small macarons
Preparation: 25 min
Cooking time: 15 min
Rest mixture: 1 h

120 g (4¼ oz) of icing sugar (confectioner's sugar)

80 g (2¾ oz) of almond flour

2 egg whites (80 g/2¾ oz)

1 pinch of salt (optional)

60 g (2 oz) of castor sugar (berry sugar)

1 pinch of yellow powdered food colouring (colouring agent)

For ganache:

70 g (2½ oz) of white chocolate

70 g (2½ oz) of banana puree

1. Make macaron shells according to the basic recipe (see p. 62).
2. Prepare ganache: in a saucepan melt the white chocolate on low heat.
3. Add banana puree. Let the mixture cool to room temperature.
4. To assemble garnish 1 macaron shell with ganache and then cover with another shell. Assemble remaining macarons accordingly.

Lychee macarons

Makes 15 to 20 small macarons
Preparation: 20 min
Cooking time: 17 min
Rest mixture: 1 h

120 g (4¼ oz) of icing sugar (confectioner's sugar)

80 g (2¾ oz) of almond flour

2 egg whites (80 g/2¾ oz)

1 pinch of salt (optional)

60 g (2 oz) of castor sugar (berry sugar)

1 pinch of pink powdered food colouring (colouring agent)

For lychee cream:

150 g (5¼ oz) of lychees

15 g (½ oz) of castor sugar (berry sugar)

1 egg

10 g (⅓ oz) of cornflour (cornstarch)

1. Make macaron shells according to the basic recipe (see p. 62).
2. Prepare lychee cream: peel and pit the lychees. Mix with castor sugar (berry sugar) and cornflour (cornstarch) to a fine consistency.
3. Transfer the mixture to a saucepan and cook for about 5 minutes on medium heat, whisking constantly until cream thickens.
4. Pour the cream into a bowl, cover with plastic wrap and let cool to room temperature.
5. To assemble garnish 1 macaron shell with lychee cream and then cover with another shell. Assemble remaining macarons accordingly.

Chocolate-spice macarons

Makes 15 to 20 small macarons
Preparation: 30 min
Cooking time: 15 min
Rest mixture: 1 h

120 g (4¼ oz) of icing sugar (confectioner's sugar)

80 g (2¾ oz) of almond flour

2 tablespoons (6 teaspoons) of unsweetened cocoa powder

2 egg whites (80 g/2¾ oz)

1 pinch of salt (optional)

60 g (2 oz) of castor sugar (berry sugar)

For ganache:

50 g (1¾ oz) of dark chocolate (semi-sweet chocolate)

35 g (1¼ oz) of spiced biscuits (speculaas or ginger snaps)

30 ml (1 fl oz) of milk

1. Make macaron shells according to the basic recipe (see p. 62), mixing the cocoa with almond flour and icing sugar (confectioner's sugar) in first step.
2. Prepare ganache: in a bowl break the spiced biscuits (speculaas or ginger snaps) into small pieces, sprinkle them with milk and let them soak. Mix to a perfectly smooth consistency.
3. In a saucepan melt the chocolate, broken into pieces, on low heat.
4. Remove from heat, blend with the spiced biscuit mixture. Let the ganache cool to room temperature.
5. To assemble garnish 1 macaron shell with ganache and then cover with another shell. Assemble remaining macarons accordingly.

Avocado macarons

Makes 15 to 20 small macarons
Preparation: 30 min
Cooking time: 20 min
Rest mixture: 1 h

120 g (4¼ oz) of icing sugar (confectioner's sugar)

80 g (2¾ oz) of almond flour

2 egg whites (80 g/2¾ oz)

1 pinch of salt (optional)

60 g (2 oz) of castor sugar (berry sugar)

1 pinch of green powdered food colouring (colouring agent)

For ganache:

100 g (3½ oz) of white chocolate

10 g (⅓ oz) of heavy whipping cream

50 g (1¾ oz) of avocado puree

1. Make macaron shells according to the basic recipe (see p. 62).
2. Prepare ganache: in a saucepan melt the white chocolate and the cream on low heat.
3. Remove from heat, stir in avocado puree. Let the ganache cool to room temperature.
4. To assemble garnish 1 macaron shell with ganache and then cover with another shell. Assemble remaining macarons accordingly.

Tomato-vanilla macarons

Makes 15 to 20 small macarons
Preparation: 30 min
Cooking time: 20 min
Rest mixture: 1 h

120 g (4¼ oz) of icing sugar (confectioner's sugar)

80 g (2¾ oz) of almond flour

2 egg whites (80 g/2¾ oz)

1 pinch of salt (optional)

60 g (2 oz) of castor sugar (berry sugar)

1 pinch of red powdered food colouring (colouring agent)

For jam:

200 g (7 oz) of ripened tomatoes

50 g (1¾ oz) of gelling sugar (jam or jelly sugar)

½ vanilla pod

1 tablespoon (3 teaspoons) of lemon juice

1. Make macaron shells according to the basic recipe (see p. 62).
2. Prepare jam: boil tomatoes for 1 minute and then dip them in a bowl of cold water. Peel and cut them into pieces. Put them in a saucepan with gelling sugar (jam or jelly sugar) and lemon juice. Heat the mixture and bring to boil. Cook for 5–7 minutes on high heat, stirring constantly.
3. Remove from heat, add seeds of vanilla pod. Let the jam cool to room temperature.
4. To assemble garnish 1 macaron shell with jam and then cover with another shell. Assemble remaining macarons accordingly.

Apple-pate macarons

Makes 15 to 20 small macarons
Preparation: 30 min
Cooking time: 20 min
Rest mixture: 1 h

120 g ($4\frac{1}{4}$ oz) of icing sugar (confectioner's sugar)

80 g ($2\frac{3}{4}$ oz) of almond flour

2 egg whites (80 g/$2\frac{3}{4}$ oz)

1 pinch of salt (optional)

60 g (2 oz) of castor sugar (berry sugar)

5 g ($\frac{1}{6}$ oz) of unsweetened cocoa powder

For filling:

2 apples

1 tablespoon (3 teaspoons) of castor sugar (berry sugar)

1 pinch of cinnamon

1 small block of duck or goose liver pate

1. Make macaron shells according to the basic recipe (see p. 62), mixing the cocoa with almond flour and icing sugar (confectioner's sugar) in first step.
2. Prepare sauce: peel apples and cut them into small cubes. Put them in a saucepan, add castor sugar (berry sugar) and simmer for 5 to 10 minutes on low heat.
3. Remove from heat, add pinch of cinnamon. Let the sauce cool to room temperature.
4. To assemble garnish 1 macaron shell with sauce. Layer 1 slice of duck or goose liver pate over sauce and then cover with another shell. Assemble remaining macarons accordingly.

Basic recipe

Makes 15 to 20 small macarons
Preparation: 20 min
Cooking time: around 12 min
Rest mixture: 1 h

120 g (4¼ oz) of icing sugar (confectioner's sugar)

80 g (2¾ oz) of almond flour

2 egg whites (80 g/2¾ oz)

1 pinch of salt (optional)

60 g (2 oz) of castor sugar (berry sugar)

1 pinch of powdered food colouring (colouring agent, which can be found in specialty baking stores)

1. Mix the icing sugar (confectioner's sugar) finely with almond flour. Sift the mixture into a bowl.

2. Whisk egg whites into firm peaks with the salt. Add the castor sugar (berry sugar) and food colouring (colouring agent), and continue whisking until meringue is very shiny.

3. Using a spatula, stir the almond mixture with egg whites by gently lifting the paste upwards. The mixture will become much brighter and a little more liquid. Be careful not to overwork the mixture to the point that it becomes completely white.

4. Using a pastry bag, make small rounds on a baking tray (baking sheet) covered with baking paper (parchment paper), spacing them evenly. Let stand for 1 hour at room temperature.

5. Preheat oven, on fan-forced (convection) option, at 150°C (300°F).

6. Bake and cook for about 12 minutes. Let the macarons cool before handling them and assemble with filling of your choice.

My advice: Macarons taste best when served within 12 to 24 hours after being made, but can be stored in an airtight container in the refrigerator for a few days.

Equivalents

LIQUID MEASUREMENTS		
METRIC	**CUP & SPOON (USED IN THIS BOOK)**	**IMPERIAL**
5 ml	1 teaspoon	⅙ fl oz
15 ml	1 tablespoon	½ fl oz
30 ml	⅛ cup	1 fl oz
60 ml	¼ cup	2 fl oz
125 ml	½ cup	4⅖ fl oz
250 ml	1 cup	8⅘ fl oz
500 ml	2 cups	⅖ quart
1 litre	4 cups	⅞ quart

SOLID MEASUREMENTS	
METRIC	**IMPERIAL**
30 g	1 oz
60 g	⅛ lbs or 2 oz
115 g	¼ lbs or 4 oz
170 g	⅜ lbs or 6 oz
225 g	½ lbs or 8 oz
454 g	1 lb or 16 oz

OVEN TEMPERATURES			
HEAT	**° CELSIUS**	**GAS MARK**	**° FAHRENHEIT**
Very low	70 °C	Gas ⅙	150 °F
Low	100 °C	Gas ¼	200 °F
	120 °C	Gas ½	250 °F
Medium	150 °C	Gas 2	300 °F
	180 °C	Gas 4	350 °F
Hot	200 °C	Gas 6	400 °F
	230 °C	Gas 8	450 °F
Very hot	260 °C	Gas 10	500 °F

hinkler

Published by Hinkler Books Pty Ltd 2011
45–55 Fairchild Street
Heatherton Victoria 3202 Australia
www.hinkler.com.au

Originally published in French as *Macarons*
978 2 8427 0997 6

Author: Marie-Laure Tombini
Photogravure: Amalthéa

ISBN: 978 1 7418 3635 6

Printed and bound in China